TERRELL JOHNICAN

A Different World

Learning from My Experiences as a First-Generation College Student

First edition

ISBN: 979-8-9868641-1-2

Cover art by Terrin Brooks
Editing by Michelle Schacht

This book was professionally typeset on Reedsy.
Find out more at reedsy.com

This book is dedicated to my family and friends who pushed me to be better, my mentors who guided me to a better life, and everyone who is resilient in creating a better future despite their past and present.

Contents

Acknowledgement

Thank you to my mother, Sonia Johnican, for raising me to be the man I am today with the resources she had. Thank you to the rest of my family, Sofia and Lester Johnican and Shirley Mouton, for always supporting me the best they can.

I would also like to thank my mentors, including Ciro Reyes, Brandie Mitchell, and Monica Floyd, who guided me, a lost, first-generation and low-income student, to a greater life and inspired me to take the path of educating others who can relate to my struggles to become a better person for themselves.

1

Introduction

First, I want to say thank you for choosing to read this book. It's my hope you can gain much insight from my perceptions of life and college. If you are reading this, you are probably:

- A newly admitted student who is considered first-generation.
- A first-generation college student who is already taking classes and is looking for help.
- A parent, guardian, family member, mentor, or a professional educator looking for different ways to support your student.
- A prospective student looking for help in the future.
- Someone simply interested in the struggles of a first-generation college student.

If you are any of these, or anybody really, you've come to the right place. I feel the information I have learned firsthand as well as through others' experiences, observations, and guidance is necessary for anyone who can impact a first-generation student in any way.

This book is designed to help you understand more about the struggles of a low-income, first generation college student and give insight to those who need help or are supporting a student facing the same battle. Throughout this book, I will explain things through my perspective and share examples from experience, but the topics that will be discussed in this book are generally the things you go through while attending college as a student like me. (To be fair, some experiences will vary based on specific locations, universities, family, personality, personal struggles, and more.) This includes going to community colleges and large universities because, although experiences may differ for various reasons, the plight of the first-generation student remains the same.

Who am I?

At this point you may be asking,

"Who is this guy and how can he possibly help me?"

Well, let me take a minute to introduce myself. I went to University of Houston-Main Campus in 2010, coming from a small town called La Marque, Texas. I was a low-income and first-generation student coming in. I was both very nervous and excited to start my new journey. I mean, attending college was so few and far between in my small town. College was more like a dream to me than something that was a normal next step after high school.

I was accepted to two colleges and denied by one, but I was excited to even get two acceptance letters. After making my decision, I prepared for the next chapter of my life ready to take place at the University of Houston. Throughout my college experience, I faced literal blood, sweat, and tears to keep up with everything, but I had mentors and guidance to help me through. Overall, I had a blessed experience from college that I know I couldn't get from anywhere else. Even through all the issues and road blocks I faced, I don't regret a thing (well, some, but we'll talk about it later).

Therefore, I have made it my duty to become a mentor for those who are like me, following in the footsteps of those who helped me. I have been working with first-generation college and high school students since I graduated college with my bachelor's in psychology, and now I've furthered my academic career in student affairs by attaining a master's in higher education administration.

I come from an area where people were not seen to go to college, and when they did, it was likely for them to come back with no degree. It is an area where if you don't get out quick enough, you're likely to be sucked into the lifestyle and you might not ever want to leave. I call it the "small town syndrome". It's a mindset that's especially hard to break when hard labor is popular, as it is in my city, and people are quick to dive into those types of jobs without even considering chasing their dreams while they are young. In a community where many of the population is low-income, most generally do not have time to chase their dreams because they need to chase money to support their families. Luckily, my mother and intermediate family encouraged me to leave our town behind to chase my dreams.

Although I have worked with and helped many first-generation students, as well as experiencing the struggle myself,

I am still working and researching to dive deeper into the mind of those who are entering the brand new and fresh environment of college. Learning never ends and growth is only stagnant when you are.

What is a first-generation student?

The term "first-generation college student" is very loosely defined. Some consider the term to refer to students who are the absolute first in their family to attend college. This means no one in the student's past generations has attended or graduated from college. Some say it describes students whose parents did not attend college, meaning any grandparents who attended college do not count. Others say students whose parents attended college but did not graduate are also first-generation. The definition I professionally see most often, and the one I will use throughout this book, is you are a first-generation student if neither of your parents have graduated college. This means if your parents have attended college and have not attained at least a bachelor's degree, which is a four-year college degree generally gained at a university, you can still be considered first-generation.

Students come in all varieties, and first-generation students are no different. Every one of us is different in our own way due to our unique personalities, experiences, family, culture, etc. After all, we are all individual beings with very individual paths. Still, there are similar experiences a typical first-generation student will have. Statistically, the first-generation student population goes through particular issues based on changing environments, isolation, problems at home, financial issues, and many more.

As a member of this population, I had to deal with adapting to the new environment of campus culture. College was brand new to me, but with a positive mindset (which I gained much later in college), I was able to conquer the land of books and beer and be proud of who I was becoming. I hope this book helps others reach that point much sooner than I did. I did not have much information about life in college, so I struggled with many things, including certain terminology, being active with campus events, opening up to people, adjusting to class schedules, etc. Coming from my small town to this big campus at the University of Houston, I had no idea how big this world was and what I had to offer it. I had to make time to find my role on campus. Finding out who I was and how I could contribute to the campus was essential in my having a sense of belonging at my university.

I was very confused about the college system as well. College lingo and definitions confused me in the beginning. My first semester, I had trouble trying to figure out where to go, who to see, what to do, and everything else in between. You may have these issues as well, but it's okay because this struggle can be short lived if you always ask questions and use your resources like I did when I finally gained the courage.

One big struggle for me was leaving my home problems at home. I felt guilty living on my nice campus, eating new foods every day in the dining hall while my family and friends were at home wondering how the next set of bills were going to be paid.

I also had to understand that some people back home did not and were never going to understand or even approve of what I was doing. Additionally, there were some people who wanted to support me but they just didn't know how because they knew absolutely nothing about college.

I faced many other struggles, like financial issues, social challenges, grades, choosing the right major, and fighting doubts of success. But guess what? I prevailed because I chose to be resilient, smart, and persistent. I gained the strength that I did not have initially to progress and graduate. You can too.

I will discuss all of these issues in this book, offering guidelines I learned through my own experiences, by observing others, and through mentoring students to assure you are happy with where you are, who you are, and the path you are going to travel.

2

A Different World

Getting your acceptance letter and knowing you are going to college can be an exhilarating moment as you prepare for a new journey in life. It can also be full of anxiety and fear, especially if you have never stepped on a campus before or you do not have other people to talk to you about college life. Most likely, first-generation students have not lived in such an environment with those who are familiar and comfortable with college life.

A college campus is a different world, and it can be just as scary as any other big change in someone's life. You're walking into another chapter of your life, not fully knowing how it will go or end. It's similar to starting a new job, having a baby, or getting married. Although anxiety might be slowly consuming you before or on your first day, realize it's necessary to take some time to adapt to your new environment, as we humans are born to do. Become familiar with your new land for a better chance to conquer it!

No Place Like Home

You're probably very used to life in your town or city and have integrated with how the environment works. You may have only gone on a few college tours or may have never even stepped on a university campus before. If this is the case, then you are probably sweating at the thought of entering a whole new world. It may feel as if you're diving into an ocean without knowing what's inside of it. But don't worry, there are ways to become familiar with your campus and not feel so disconnected from the environment you have stepped foot in.

First, we must recognize at the very beginning, unless you are sick of your home, you will be homesick. Sometimes both feelings are relevant. I had the choice to start at a community college, which is usually cheaper and less threatening than going to a large university. I would have been able to stay in my hometown and get my basic classes out of the way at a cheaper cost, then transfer to a university to finish off my major studies. But there was one flaw in that plan. I was simply sick of my home. Sick of the environment I was in. Sick of dealing with financial struggles. Sick of the life I was living in high school ignorance and sick of the small-town blues. I wanted much more out of my life and, most importantly, I wanted a fresh start. At the time, I knew I had to leave my community to have any chance at the type of success I aimed for, financial stability and a promising career.

In high school, I was in a program called Upward Bound, a TRIO program designed to help first-generation and low-income students receive the college preparation they would otherwise not experience. With the TRIO program, I traveled to different colleges and universities and was able to see outside the realm of my county. I was so blown away by the different world of the university and was very excited to get there. So, when I was ultimately accepted into the University of Houston, I lost my mind.

But, when I got there, I was nervous. I was nervous because the feeling of stepping on the campus as a freshman is way different than walking into a classroom as a high school student. I'd upgraded. I felt freedom and power, but that came with responsibility, and responsibility mixed with the unknown becomes fear and anxiety. I began to realize how different the college environment is especially at University of Houston which at the time was very large and the third most diverse university in the nation. Remember, I came from a predominantly black, low-income, small town. This new environment certainly was not home.

I was already introverted and terrified of approaching people. I had to figure out most things, like where to find my classes and how to use the college's database, by myself. But the key to taking action and adapting to college was to first come to terms with the fact that this was not home.

It took me a while to truly detach from my home world because I was raised close to Houston in Galveston County, which is still a part of the greater Houston area. Unlike those students who lived father away, I could go home anytime I wanted with the help of my grandfather and his truck. Of course, it's great to see family and go home sometimes, but I was abusing that power and using it as a cushion to escape having to deal with the awkward and difficult life I was experiencing in college. I had to realize that in order to move forward I had to let some things go and leave some people behind. I had to alleviate my worries and get rid of the cultural cushion I had at home. Even then, I still went home often, just not as much as I did initially, and I did not use it to escape the fear of my new environment.

In order to make it in college and the world as a first-generation student, you must be able to face those fears and jump the nest. Especially if you feel like nothing is for you at home, you won't be doing yourself a favor by not accepting the truth of being in a new land and having to adapt to its surroundings. You will be more than okay if you stand strong and take action.

You May Seem Alone

One of the biggest struggles I dealt with in my first semester was the inescapable feeling of being alone. College was a brand-new environment for me. I knew no one on campus. Yes, I was looking for a fresh start, but I forgot that a fresh start meant erasing everything and starting over. I never had a problem with making friends if I was approached, but I was not good at socializing or taking the initiative to introduce myself to others.

I had a roommate during my first year and so forth, and he was cool, but you cannot assume a roommate will turn into a good friend.[1] I had no issues with my first roommate, but we never did anything together or even spoke more than small talk outside of the dorm room. He wasn't even there for the first few weeks, so I definitely started my college experience completely

---

[1] I did have other roommates while I was in college. I connected with most of them in some way, but some roommates were also distant or simply busy living their own lives. There is nothing wrong with not making best friends with your roommates, as long as spaces, rules, and considerations are respected and communication otherwise is made clear and quickly.

alone. The point is, if you are feeling alone, you have to push past that feeling and reach out. Approach people, and if you cannot, I'm sure there are plenty of social events, organizations, and campus activities that can give you a reason to socialize with your fellow peers.

Explore

Thankfully, my sense of wonder caused me to walk outside of the four-cornered walls which were my dorm to explore the campus. In my first week, I took time to walk around my campus, find where my classes would be held, and observe my new environment. The more I explored the campus, the less frightened I felt about the university's environment. Don't get me wrong, I was still uncomfortable due to social anxiety, but at least I was familiar with my surroundings. That definitely eased some stress for me.

Speaking of social anxiety, I had a very hard time being in areas of high social activity. I'm not sure why I was so afraid to talk to new people, but I would go out of my way and find alternate routes to my destinations to avoid large social scenes. I used to go hungry before I would enter a packed dining hall and if I was even a second late to class, I would turn around only because I did not want everyone looking at me while I walked into class. My anxiety has gotten better, but it was especially bad my first year.

What I learned is if you feel like you are in a brand-new environment and it's bringing you anxiety, becoming familiar with your surroundings and exploring the campus as much as possible makes it better. It's likely that you'll feel more comfortable in a place you are familiar with and you're liable to find a building, study room, organization, or special place that you feel you can go to for creating an ambiance of your version of home.

Though, while you are on your path for feeling at home, you also need to understand that you are not at home and you'll need to spend time being one with your campus. The goal is to create a home at campus, not to cling to and obsess over how home used to be. This may not be everyone's issue, but I do believe, whether you liked your old home environment or not, you were familiar with it, and sensing the shock factor of a university especially as a first-generation student can definitely make you feel homesick.

Parents

I will talk about tips and experiences for the student throughout the entire book, but I am also including a part in every chapter where I speak to parents about what they can do to support and strengthen their child's chances in surviving college. In this case of adapting to a new home, parents, you must let your child free.

I know you'll miss your child when they move to the big leagues and you will want to call them every day, all day. And I'm not telling you that's wrong! But, please understand that the more your child sticks to home, the lesser the chance they'll have at getting comfortable with their new environment.

Like I mentioned before, there is no problem with going back home and meeting with family and friends as long as it does not become a desperate escape from the new environment. Let your child experience new things and take time to find themselves. Let them be free by checking on them, but not smothering them.

Provide support when they need it, but do not guide their every step as if they are you. We as humans are born to adapt, and eventually we all find our own way. Sometimes all we need is a little push. This is your child's time to develop his or her true self. Watch from a distance and step in if you think they're reaching a ledge they won't survive falling from.

3

What's Your Role?

Finding your role on campus is just as important as getting good grades and turning in your work. Finding yourself and your role is essential in having a sense of belonging on your campus, adapting to your environment, and finding friends who connect with you.

People tend to gravitate to those they relate to when finding themselves on campus. For me, the more I ventured out for events and organizations that piqued my interest, the more friends with similar interests I found. This is why finding your way is so important.

By being involved with your campus, you'll also have the benefit of getting better grades and having a smoother academic journey. Why? Because you work harder for things you believe in, and if you find your role and love the campus you are involved in, you are more likely to be involved in your studies. You will be more motivated to play your role and be a successful part of the college you are enrolled in. This includes finding friends to study with and having a better overall mood due to a new sense of belonging. As long as you do not take more than you know you can handle, you should be okay.

I personally found my role in music, poetry, and being a first-generation college student. I found organizations that appealed to me as a first-generation student, I attended open mic events to meet other poets and artists, and I searched for people who shared the same love for music. However, this did not happen fast; it took me some time to stop acting like an outcast and find friends. It took time to look inside myself and search for who I was and what I wanted. Growth at college is a long process. Do not expect to have everything together in your freshman year. But I promise you it will come. It's all part of the journey.

You Are Not an Outcast

Julian Stainback, a fellow first-generation, low-income student, stated in his blog,

> *Of the 56 students in my high school class, there were only a few people that went on to attend a four-year university. The rest either picked up jobs, went to community college or joined the military.*[2]

As a first-generation or low-income college student, having the assumption that people like you don't normally go down the path you chose can make you feel like an outcast. When I first started college, I felt like I didn't belong. I felt like an outcast, so I began to act like an outcast. I wouldn't talk to anyone and I

---

[2] "Column: My experience as a low-income, first generation student," *The State News*, https://statenews.com/article/2022/03/column-my-experience-as-a-first-gen-student?ct=content_open&cv=cbox_latest

would rarely leave my dorm. When I did, I would do everything alone. This was a terrible way to live and it slowly destroyed me inside. My roommate was rarely in our dorm, so I felt like I had it all to myself. I'm sure a lot of people would have seen this as a good thing, but I never felt so alone before that moment.

I went to a very diverse university, but even if you aren't at such a campus, you should still be able to find someone to relate. You are not the outcast you think you are. There is someone on campus who matches your demographics, major, study methods, hobbies, etc. You just have to get out there and make yourself available.

Define Your Own Success

After failing some classes in my freshman year, I was put on probation. I went in with a little college classroom experience due to dual credit, which is college credit gain in high school, but unfortunately not enough to positively affect my grades at University of Houston.

> *Colleges have specific criteria for student enrollment, like minimum GPA and credit load requirements. If students don't meet those criteria, they may be put on academic probation. Academic probation is a period of time in which students must improve their academic standing by meeting or making evident progress toward their school's eligibility criteria. Students on academic probation typically have to:*
>
> *Pass a specified number of credits*
> *Earn a good GPA (determined by the school)*
> *Meet with academic advisors during their probationary*

period[3]

Normally, freshmen who are failing go on warning because the university understands that it's their first year, but since I came in with college credits they must have figured I knew what I was doing and put me right on probation. I wish I would have been told that in dual credit. In a probationary period, you can continue to take classes, but you have to make a minimum grade point average every semester until your cumulative, or overall, GPA reaches the minimum required to get you off of probation. That can vary from school to school, but that was my situation.

It honestly took me until my junior year of college to get that probation off of me. It was always looming over me, threatening my mind with the possibility of going back home a failure. It's definitely not a good position to be in, but I still made it out, graduated, and found a career with opportunities.

I say all of this to paint you an image of my academic "success" at the time. One of the few things I can blame my roadblocks on was my unwillingness to find my sense of belonging on campus. When I began to join organizations, create circles of friends, and attend events tailored to my liking, I did better in school. This was because I felt like I was meant to be there rather than believing that I did not belong.

College is a great time to discover who you are and get a feel of what role you can play in society. Do not waste that time being an outcast. I'm very sure you are not the only one on your

---

[3] "Academic Probation in College: What It Is and How to Get Back on Track," *Accredited Schools Online,* https://www.accreditedschoolsonline.org/resour ces/academic-probation/

campus feeling that way. Step out of your box, including your dorm room, and find your role. You relate to those around you more than you think.

Although you relate to those around you in specific ways, you are also unique in many ways. College is the best time to find your identity as this may actually be the freest you will ever be in terms of availability and exploration options. As a college student, even though you may have certain responsibilities at school and even have some at home, you generally will have time to explore student life and take opportunities to try new things. Of course, there are many exceptions, but you get the idea. Use this time at school to experiment and find yourself. Don't be afraid to step outside of your comfort zone; college is the best time to venture out into other things.

Be a Better You

Believe in what you are strong at, what others may lack, and vice versa. This means you will see others and compare yourself to them, especially if you are considered low-income. Without even knowing them or their personal struggles, I used to look at people who seemed more privileged and feel bad about myself because I felt like I did not have what they had. Don't fall for smoke and mirrors. Everyone is struggling with something. It may not be money for everyone. It could be family, social life, mental disorders, school, etc. I say all of this to encourage you to stop comparing yourself to others.

In today's world of social media, we tend to judge ourselves based on what we see in others, not realizing that other people almost always only show the good things in their life and rarely show their pain, unless it unconsciously slips of course, but that's for another book. As first-generation students, we are already told that we are behind other students, and we have to play catch up. We cannot let that assumption break us down and stop up from achieving our best goals.

Define your own success. Do not try to chase what other people consider success because they are simply not you. If you consider success to be an artist with a painting in a gallery, then so be it. If your thought of success in starting your own business, then so be it. If you wish to succeed by simply earning a degree to prove that you could do it, then so be it. You will be much happier chasing your own goals then somebody else's. Find your role and find your goals.

Get Involved

One of the best ways to find your role on campus is to get involved. It's like a domino effect. You'll begin to attend events, get free stuff like shirts and food, and join organizations. Then you'll start to have a sense of belonging and an appreciation of the campus or at least the place you find yourself the majority of your time. Before you know it, you'll be active, social, experienced, and will have found your role on campus.

If you're familiar with psychology, you may have heard about Maslow's hierarchy of needs. The hierarchy of needs describes and orders the most important things humans need to live a fulfilling life. Things like physiological and safety needs are included, but what's more specific to this subject is the third most important concept in the hierarchy of needs list—love and a sense of belonging. Once you get involved on your campus, you'll feel like you truly belong there. You'll start to connect who you are with the college or university you are attending.

And in turn, you'll likely improve in your academics. Yes, I said it. Becoming more involved on your campus is one of the greatest ways to get better grades. Creating your sense of belonging, finding your role, and getting comfortable on campus will not only give you motivation to do your classwork but provide opportunities to improve your grades. Events, peer study, campus resources, and more will become widely available to you. Check out this chart from NSSE explaining the positive correlation between first-year students' sense of belonging and intent to return to the institution for the next year.

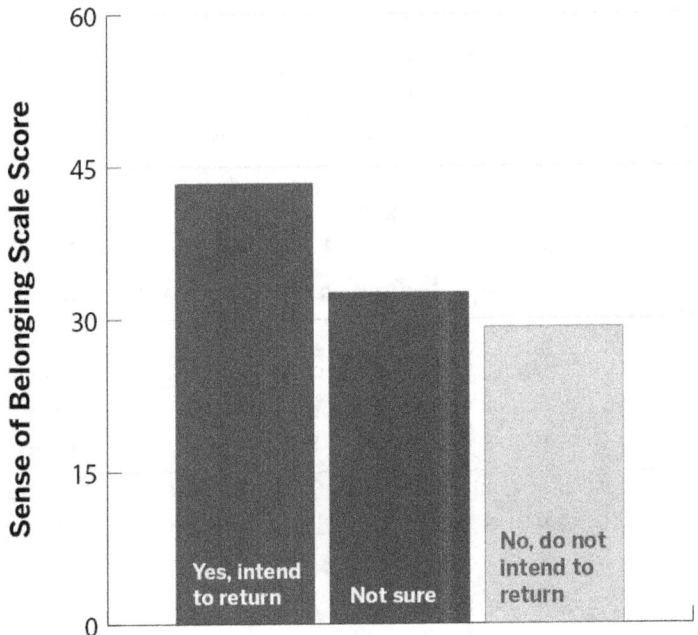

Figure 1. First-Year Students' Sense of Belonging by Intent to
Return to the Institution[4]

Along with that sense of belonging, you will also develop a
healthy work/life balance. Staying in the four corners of your

4   "Building a Sense of Community For All" NSSE, Center for Postsecondary
    Research
        Indiana University School of Education, Assessed August 23, 2022,
    https://nsse.indiana.edu/research/annual-results/belonging-story/index.h
    tml

dorm room deep into your textbook or laptop all the time will drain you of your soul and crush your work ethic. You will eventually be so tired of working that you will be mentally and sometimes even physically exhausted. This is called burnout. Burnout is very real, and for the sake of your mental health, memories, and overall college experience, learn to get out, take a break, and participate.

Personally, I was very introverted and dealt with social anxiety. I nearly lost my mind being afraid to participate in college events and feeling caged to my dorm. I did not truly enjoy my college experience for the first year and gained friends only when I gathered the courage to finally experience my campus. That was easily one of the best moves I made during my university journey. I became more involved, had more resources, gained lifetime friends, and made lasting connections—all of which saved me from dropping out of college.

Enjoy Your Experience

Before you know it, you'll be walking on the stage and shaking the hand of the university president. Four years may seem like a long time in a young or ambitious life, but those four years will go very, very fast. Please enjoy your freedom as a college student while you have it.

While I was in college, even though my friends back at home still had apartments and threw parties, they also worked at jobs they hated and often drank away their problems. As you may or may not realize, undergraduate college life is a breath of fresh air compared to real life in terms of freedom, especially for low-income and first-generation students.

You are in control of how you spend your time on campus. You can get up and direct your life every day. You can choose to take advantage of the opportunities on campus or you can stay shelled in your own tiny world. You can sleep in or stay up all night if you like. Feeling bored? Go to the student center! Need a place to study? I'm sure your college or university has hundreds of places where you can study and learn. All I'm saying is your time at university will provide you with the resources and range of choices you'll want to experience during your young adult years. Use your time at school wisely.

I took college courses at a community college while I was in high school before I went to the University of Houston. They called it dual credit. I was able to gain college credit while in high school to get a head start in college. I still graduated college a semester late, but those extra fifteen credits gave me a great cushion for my early academic slip ups at University of Houston.

The first professor I ever had at community college said something simple, but it was something I never forgot. He said,

"College was undoubtedly the best time of my entire life."

This struck me as exciting! But as I progressed through freshman year and fell into depression due to my lack and fear of experiencing the campus, I couldn't help but to remember his statement and my initial reaction. I thought,

"That professor has lived a full life. He's traveled, taught, learned, been married, and so much more. For him to say college was above all of that must mean it is something

big. I cannot waste the possible best time of my life doing nothing."

And that, my readers, was the moment I became active.

Parents

Make sure your kids are active at school. Ask them what they are doing on campus. Be interested in their activities and experiences. Encourage their participation and involvement. This will go a long way and will help your child develop themselves more than just academically. You will probably see changes in your children as they explore the world, but make sure they stay on a positive track as they experience student life. Seek to find a balance of letting them live and learn. Too many restrictions can harm your child from learning; they may become too dependent or sheltered when life beyond college occurs.

You can also look at their college's website for organizations or events you think they will enjoy and let them know about them. Sometimes if a student is trapped in their own bubble, they won't recognize the opportunities right in front of them. To ensure a great college experience for your children, encourage them to be a part of the college they're attending.

4

Keep Up

In order to have a successful college experience, you must be aware of academic system and terminologies that come with college and be willing to learn them. You don't want to make bad decisions that may be irreversible because you did not have enough information to know that was not a wise choice. Being a first-generation student means you may not know many ways of the university system because maybe no one was there to teach you. Maybe the people back at home doesn't know about the system because they did not go to college themselves. That leaves you with the responsibility of learning and keeping up with how college works for yourself. I'll be giving some tips and terms to remember, but it is your job to be on top of things so you can avoid making easy mistakes.

Attack Confusion

Give a man a fish and you'll feed him for a day. Teach a man to fish and you'll feed him for a lifetime. But what about the man teaching himself how to fish? Sometimes the answers aren't obvious and there isn't someone to help at the time. Unfortunately, being a first-generation student may mean that your family may not know the answers either. This can cause confusion and discouragement in your freshman year. But guess what? You have the power to change that.

Take it upon yourself to attack confusion by researching answers and never stop asking questions. People are set up on your campus to answer any questions you have and get the answers you need. Even your college website should give you some type of answer depending on how much you search the website. (You can usually find your college website by typing your college's acronym and ".edu" in the URL. If the college's URL is different or you are having trouble finding it, then a simple Google search should suffice.) Basically, don't just accept the fact that you don't know anything. You are in college to learn, so learn college! When asked about what questions first generation students should be asking, Nancy Milne, owner of Milne Collegiate Consulting, commented on Unigo.com,

> *Beyond the typical applicant questions, first gen students may want to inquire about support services and financial aid awards targeted to their population. Being the first in a family to pave the way through college you may feel like you are on your own or your family may be so excited about your matriculation that you feel overwhelmed either way. Having someone as a mentor or advisor to check in with can help reduce any stress in this new experience. There is no such thing as a dumb question, only an unasked one; so don't hesitate to seek out help. I guarantee that you are not the only first gen student on campus and*

you should be thrilled that you've made it that far.[5]

College Operations

Proper preparation prevents poor performance. You need to understand how college operates in order to not become lost in the system. Understand the terminologies, the processes, and the responsibilities you have as a student to make sure you stay in good standing.

This means you need to learn how your GPA works, what's your academic standing, how credit hours are calculated, and a lot more. Additionally, in order to adapt to the campus culture, you must learn the campus lingo. First-generation students generally do not have translators, those who can teach the college language, before arriving on campus. This means they must find a translator or mentor on campus, or do the research themselves. So let me be a bit of a translator for you. There is so much to learn when having the college experience, but I will explain some of the more important things for you.

One of the most important aspects of the university system to understand is credit hours. Understanding credit hours is not only necessary to keep you on track for graduation; they can also affect things like financial aid and housing. Credit hours refers to how much credit you will receive for passing a class. It's generally determined by the hours you are intended to attend class in a week. For example, if you have a class where you spend three hours a week in learning, that class will be considered three credit hours. That's usually the case in classes,

---

[5] Nancy Milne, comment on Unigo.com, "What Questions Should First Gen Students Be Asking?"

but there are also one, two, or four credit courses, depending on time spent in class or college policies.

Taking twelve credit hours in a semester is considered being a fulltime student, while six is considered halftime. Remember when I mentioned that credit hours can affect financial aid? The amount you receive in financial aid can change depending on your credit hour status. If you're only halftime or even slightly less than full time, it can lower the amount of financial aid you get. This allows for the prevention of scams and over awarding students who have lower tuition prices than others due to having less classes. So, it is important to know how many credit hours you are taking each semester and how it's affecting your financial aid.

I also recommend that you research your university's policies on academic standing. God forbid, if you find yourself in the process of having your academic standing reviewed, you will not enter as confused and lost as I was.

Generally, there is good academic standing, academic warning, and academic probation. Academic probation usually occurs when your grade point average (GPA) goes under a 2.0. This means you are being more closely looked at and you will follow a different process in registering for classes. This is what I went through my freshman year. I assumed that because I was a freshman I would have gone under academic warning. I quickly found out that I was put under academic probation because I came in at my university with 19 college credit hours from the dual credit program in my high school, therefore, counting me as a transfer student instead of a first-year freshman. This is my personal experience, but it is a fair warning for you to keep up with your grades so you don't have to dance on the line of failure like I did.

First, as I was on academic probation, it was a requirement for me to see an academic advisor to check if I was staying on track. When I say requirement, I mean that I was locked from registering for classes until I accomplished this task. It was that serious.

I was stuck in academic probation until I raised my cumulative GPA above a 2.0. Until then, every semester I needed at least a semester GPA of 2.0 to prevent a worse consequence. If I failed to receive a semester 2.0 GPA, then I would be forced to take a semester off, therefore taking more time away from graduation. If I was to come back and continue to make semester GPA's below 2.0, the next mandatory time off would be a year and the final time would be expulsion from the college. So overall, you must maintain a semester GPA of 2.0 until you reach over 2.0 in your cumulative GPA. Only then will you successfully return back to a good academic standing. Fortunately, I was able to return back to good standing after a year or so in academic probation. It's okay if you find yourself on academic probation. Just focus, prioritize your classes, understand the academic standing process at your college, and please don't be afraid to ask for help if you need it.

There is much more to learn about the way universities and colleges operate, but that will be another book for another day. This book is about your survival, and we have much more to get into for your success.

Parents

Learn with your child! Please, by all means, do not let your children learn about the college process on their own. You can research this information like they can. If your child comes to you with a question, instead of admitting defeat by not giving answers, offer to brainstorm and find the solution together. I promise this will go a long way with your child because they will know they have support back at home and will be happier in learning the process of college and the language of the campus culture.

5

Think Long-Term

For a first-generation student, college can be a trying time. You have to deal with adjusting to college and may also be dealing with struggles at home. I personally struggled with both, sorrowing in the fact that I could not help out financially at home while I was in college.

I would often think,

> *"If I was already working or lived closer to home, my mother may not be having the lights off and sitting with an empty refrigerator."*

Fortunately, many of my mentors advised me to think of the long-term benefits of my academic career and to not worry so much about things I could not change. Because they instilled that in me, it is what I will instill in you with this chapter. Think long-term, enjoy your college experience, and think about what you can do for your family by building on a foundation instead of building on nothing.

Resilience Is Key

Most first-generation students are also low-income, and if that is you, you will surely find roadblocks in you and your family's finances, in college and back at your own home. Even though I dined every day from a meal plan my freshman year, I still had no money to my name and a limited supply of food whenever the dining hall was closed or unavailable. The only money I had was whatever was left in my financial aid refund and the extra cash for outside food that came out of my meal plan. I had no money coming from my mother or any other family member. It was not because they did not want to help, but simply because they could not.

My family was dealing with their own financial struggles at home. Nothing changed back home when I left. If anything, it was worse because I did not have the income I was making with my teenage job. This hurt me in ways I could never imagine. There were phone calls about the electricity being shut off. Payday loans had to be taken out and renewed over and over again. Old cars were breaking down and my family was losing transportation in a town where buses or taxis weren't really a thing. This exhausted me. I couldn't focus on school work because I was focused on money. Money I could not obtain. Things I could not change.

If you can relate this, know that even if you can't change your family's situation now, you are working to have that chance later. You are taking a path to greater opportunities. The college years will fly by, and if you make the right moves, you could give back to yourself, your family, and maybe even your community. Just hold on; you are strong and so is your family. Resilience is key.

A study that focuses on resilience & emotional intelligence mentions:

> *A moderate to high resilience may enhance the performance of first generation students during college life, permitting them to achieve their goals and handle the pressures of exams, projects, classes, economic stressors, social pressure and other factors that may distract a college student.*

The same study shows results indicating that first generation college students had higher levels of resilience than non-first generation college students.[6]

Lighten The Load

There are ways to lighten the financial load. One of the ways, like I mentioned, is having a meal plan. Most universities offer several meal plans with different options, varying in forms of how many dining visits you have or how much money you want dedicated to other foods on campus, like fast food restaurants. These meal plans are your ticket for food. Make sure you research your campus meal plans options to ensure you are fed when you need to be. Even if you only choose a modest plan, at least you are guaranteed a meal within your meal plan boundaries.

People joke about eating ramen noodles and Hot Pockets all

---

[6] Andreina Alvarado, Alexandru Spatariu, & Christine Woodbury. "Resilience & Emotional Intelligence between First Generation College Students an Non-First Generation College Student," *Focus on Colleges, Universities, and Schools* 11, no. 1 (2017): 1-8

throughout college, which is true to some extent, but I find that statement more false than true. I've tried so many different dishes and foods in my dining hall back at the University of Houston. I would have never expanded my taste buds this far in my old environment. I probably would have never known those certain foods existed. There were international dishes, new pastas, omelets, and desserts for days. If that doesn't satisfy your taste buds, you can just get a classic pizza or cereal. Mix that cereal with chocolate milk if you want! Who's going to stop you? It's up to you, but at least you will be fed. Now, that does not quite solve your family's situation back at home, but your family may be pleased to know that you're not starving while being so far away.

Work-study and seasonal jobs are also great ways to keep some income in your pocket without sacrificing too much study time. Work-study is a grant that allows you to work a part-time job on campus that lets you study in its downtime. The jobs are rarely hard, which is done on purpose so you can have time to study. Every work-study job is different, so take that last sentence with a grain of salt, but that is usually the idea. Some jobs may have a full workload for you while others may be really laid back.

For example, I've had work-study jobs in student success programs and dean's offices that were very simple and afforded me the perfect time to focus and get schoolwork done. In my last two years, I worked at a game room on campus, which did not give me time to study, but I traded that for great memories. I can honestly say that job made for some of the best times of my college experience. It was so fun and it forced me to meet new people all the time. Plus, because it was a fun environment, I was able to loosen up and be myself. If you can, get a work-study job. Make sure you ask for it when you apply for financial aid and talk to whatever department that handles student jobs to check for availability. For me, that department was career services.

Another option for income is seasonal jobs. These are jobs you can come back to during winter and summer breaks while you take classes in the fall and spring. You can make money during your break with the extra time you have, even if you take a few summer classes.

I was lucky enough to have a solid position at Moody Gardens back home where my supervisor always saved a spot for me during my school breaks. I did a pretty good job there, which kept me going. I was able to support my mother and build some money for myself through the breaks. If you can, find a job that allows seasonal work, and if you are a high school graduate with a job in your last summer before school starts, make sure you make a good impression. They may want to keep you as a seasonal employee.

Family Financials

Another thing you may deal with, and you may already be aware of, is your family's financial struggles. If you are low-income, your family's financial struggles will not suddenly undergo a significant change unless someone else in your family makes a change. Remember, you are thinking long-term in your education. With the right moves, you will be able to help out your family and more, but it definitely won't be during your freshman year.

I went into a deep depression my first year at school because I felt helpless. I could not support my mother and other family members like I wanted to. I would get phone calls about the lights in the apartment being turned off, car problems, issues with paying rent, and more. And all I could do was listen.

It was devastating for me as the only man in the house to hear that and not be able to do anything. I started work early at age sixteen to help out my mother, then I went to college in hope that I could break the vicious cycle and save my family from poverty. But I couldn't think long-term when my mother didn't have food in the kitchen now.

My mentors, thank God for them, continued to tell me to not worry about things I could not change and to continue to think about the big picture. It was a very hard concept to understand, but I knew if I wanted to survive college, I needed to understand that. If not, the guilt inside me would eat me alive and I would not have the energy or will to continue.

I say this because I want to relay the information my mentors gave me to you, no matter how hard a pill it is to swallow. You have a mission. Right now, your mission is not back at home. Your mission is to graduate for a chance at a better future for you and possibly them as well.

I'm not saying to completely disregard your home struggles, but rather to understand why you should focus on the future and your personal situations rather than the situations at home. Be there for your family and home friends, listen to them, and help when you can, but please do not stress yourself out trying to save everyone. It's not your time yet. You will return as the hero soon enough.

It's Time to Be a Bit Selfish

This section is distinctly for those who are younger, maybe straight out of high school, and are stepping into a new experience. Look, you are young and experiencing a new world. It's about time to start thinking about yourself.

If you are like me, you probably spent a lot of your teenage years trying to keep your family afloat. For me, it was financially, but it could vary in many ways for each person. To be that young and worried about bills, rent, and other expenses, it was no shock that it carried over to my college years. What made it even worse is I didn't have enough time for a full-time job; school was challenging enough as it was. When I went to college, I went from supporting my family to being incapable of helping.

I mentioned this feeling earlier when discussing thinking long-term, but I want to stress the importance of looking forward and thinking about your growth. When the struggles are real, it's hard to think about yourself, but how can you really grow if you're only living for others? I'm not saying you shouldn't be caring, but I want you to focus on your inner growth and think about how you want your life to progress. Especially if there's not much you can do about the situation at home. Think about the future. Think about the investment. Think about yourself.

Self-sabotage and Self-fulfilling Prophecy

This was a major hindrance for me. Just ask one of my mentors, Ms. Floyd. She has told me many times that I have a self-destructive habit where every time I start doing well, I somehow can't believe it or cast doubt over myself, so I push the handles forward and plummet straight to the ground.

This caused so much more pain in my college journey than there should have been. I couldn't wrap my head around the fact that I, a young black boy from a disadvantaged background, was capable of accomplishing what I was, and I often lost confidence in my abilities. Friends and mentors always seemed to find the value in me when I couldn't find the value in myself. I just want to point this out to make sure you know that you are capable, you have a right to be where you are, and you have more value in this world than you may think. Keep going and believe in yourself.

Don't Worry About Things You Can't Change

I know this is easier said than done, believe me, but this is something you have to overcome. I spent so much time worrying about issues at home, I lost sight of the issues I had in college. I lost sight of the main goal. I lost sight of why I left home in the first place, which was to gain a better education and a more promising future for me and everyone I cared for.

One of my other mentors, Ms. Brandie, would often say

> *"Obstacles are going to happen; that is not your story. Your story is how you overcome the obstacles."*

We cannot focus on obstacles too much because we then lose sight of the goal, especially if those obstacles are something we can't do anything about because they're always lingering over our heads. We must learn how to overcome the obstacles we can, learn to omit the worry over the outside obstacles we cannot change, and stay focused on the main goal, which is to graduate.

Parents

I know you want your children to succeed. I know they may have been a solution to your problems before. However, you must let them live and develop themselves. Keep them updated about what is going on at home, but don't drown them in your problems.

I love my mother to death, but it only depressed me more to hear all of the issues she was having back home and how I could do nothing about it at the time because I was in college.

Your children may wish they could do more for you, like they may or may not have been able to before college. I supported the household at age sixteen when I started work. There was no father in my home, and my mother was considered low-income, so I did my part and pitched in on some of the bills. When I left for college, I couldn't help as much as I used to and it hurt. But I had to think about the future, and because I did so, I now can help her way more than I was able to at sixteen.

I say all that just to say that sometimes we have to trust the process and think long-term. If things are done right, it will be highly beneficial for your child and whoever your child loves enough to support.

6

Have Faith In Your Path

We can all lose hope sometimes when the path seems rocky and we're not sure if we can make it though. In times like this, you must keep hope alive. You must have faith in your support system. Have faith in your passions and career choice. Most importantly, have faith in your own abilities, adaptations, and growth.

Your Support System

There were countless times in my college journey where I lost confidence and faith in receiving my bachelor's degree. Many aspects and variables contributed to that feeling of lost hope. Sometimes it was the environment, sometimes it was social, sometimes it was financial, and sometimes it was intrapersonal. But overall, it was me not supporting myself and my own goals.

This is where my support system came in. TRIO's Student Support Services, the Urban Experience Program, and family and friends kept me going when I wanted to go no longer. My family provided emotional support, my friends provided social support, and my mentors at the programs I mentioned provided me with resilience and wisdom. I don't think I would have made it without these people in my life. I'm sure I'm not the only one to feel this way. In fact, first-generation college student Isabel Banda mentioned on The Century Foundation website:

> *As a first time student, everything from choosing classes and navigating financial aid to finding housing can be very difficult and affect student success and persistence in college. I was fortunate enough to have the support of the TRIO Student Support Services Program (SSSP) to assist with any barriers that I faced as a first generation college student.*
>
> *College access and success programs like TRIO's SSSP provide significant and necessary contributions to the goal of improving higher education attainment for students from underrepresented groups.[7]*

It is a necessity that you find your support system. It may not be like mine, but it will be yours and how you want it to be. Keep positive friends around and stay away from those that bring negative energy even when you reach out to support them. Hopefully, your family wants to see you succeed, and if not, I'm sure there is someone in this world who cares about you enough to want to see you make it. Take advantage of the support and student success programs on your campus that can help keep you afloat. Don't try to do this by yourself. Get help

---

[7] Isabel Banda, "Why Support Services for First-Generation, Low-Income Students Matter," last modified July 27, 2021, https://tcf.org/content/com mentary/support-services-first-generation-low-income-students-matter/? agreed=1

and extrinsic motivation.

"I don't know what's going on, but I'm proud of you."

I love my family and my mother to no end, but as a first-generation student I found it hard to talk to them about college issues. When I was on probation slipping in my grades and moving around like I had failed before failing, I would sometimes call my mother to express my frustrations.

My mother is very sweet and she is always there for support. Unfortunately, because she has never been to a university, she often has no idea what I'm talking about. This causes her to give me the only support she can.

"I'm proud of you. You're doing great."

This is why that hurts. I love her for doing so, but how can you explain how "not great" you're doing to someone who has never experienced your issues? All she, and many others from my home environment, saw was a black boy from the hood going to college and striving in life. Inside, I was struggling and trying my hardest to not drop out and pursue something else. Every time she would say,

"I'm proud of you"

I would think,

"There's nothing to be proud of. I'm a few inches close to being kicked out, I feel like I don't belong, and all of my friends are living their lives back at home while I sulk in

this self-made cage I called my dorm room."

Here's how you can adapt to this issue. *Employ understanding.* Understand and accept that the ones back home who support you cannot support you in some ways, but will support you how they can. Sometimes that can just be emotional support.

Also understand there are many types of academic support and guidance within the university or college system that have resources and programs you can take advantage of. I personally gained most of that help from the TRIO Challenger Program and the Urban Experience Program at my university. Those programs gave me answers when my mother could not, and my mother gave me emotional support when the programs were too busy to do so. It's all about assigning peoples' roles in your support network and understanding their strengths and weaknesses.

Non-Traditional Career Paths

Majors like engineering, law, criminal justice, pre-med, and a few others are usually crowned as the "go-to" majors for promising careers. But what about the non-traditional majors like creative writing, art, or philosophy for examples? These and most other liberal arts majors are sometimes ridiculed for being a "poor choice" in terms of sustaining a career and financial future.

I majored in psychology, which is one of those non-traditional paths. It's a very broad major with no clear path of a job or career. Most people say you will absolutely need to go to a graduate school after earning this undergraduate degree or risk not getting a job. Hearing these things constantly brought upon a certain amount of anxiety when I considered my choice of major.

Fast forward to now, I've found a career in education that has grown significantly since then. Although I started small when I graduated with what was basically a paid internship, the point is there was at least some type of path for me. It's all about effort mixed with planning, opportunity, consistency, and resilience.

Believe in your path. If the major you choose is your desire or passion, you may be happier pursuing a career in that field that earns you possibly a little less money than working in a field you don't like for a little more money. You may even achieve your desired income with enough work and opportunity.

As a first-generation and possibly low-income student, you might think,

> *"Man, that engineer or lawyer money sounds good. I've never even seen that type of money."*

I thought that way multiple times through college. But even though I still occasionally think about my career decisions, I do not regret my path one bit. I enjoy where I am, and I cannot see myself doing anything else career-wise. I can see myself hating an engineering job and being overwhelmed as a lawyer. And honestly, I've never seen the money I make now as a middle-class citizen. I'm happy to be where I am and still work in a career field that I love.

Do not choose your path for the money, no matter how good it looks and how much you think you need it. Think on this instead. What do you want to give to this world? What makes you happy or at least content? What career would you see yourself being proud of having had after you retire? What impact do you want to make in this world? Pursue that path. Bottom line.

For Those Who Don't Support You

As you may or may not know, you cannot expect everyone to understand or support your path. Some may disagree with the path of higher education and some may disagree with your choice of career. Some people may be indifferent, and some people may be too deep in their own lives to care. Some people may be jealous, and some people just may not like you personally. None of this matters.

You are going through this path for you. As long as you know your goals and benefits, do not let other voices of assumptions and ignorance stop you from achieving what you've set out to achieve. Instead, focus on your positive support and you will be okay. Do not let non-supporters make you anxious about your decisions. You are strong enough to make and adapt to your own choices. Do you see how short this section is? That's how much they matter. On to the next thing.

Parents

I urge you to support your students the best way you know how and be aware if your student is struggling. My mother could not support me academically or financially, but I always knew she was rooting for me on the sidelines. Even when I knew she had no idea how deep in trouble I was and that stressed me out even more, I was at least grateful I had a parent who still wanted to see me do the best I could.

Even if you don't know how to support your child in the most effective way, a simple checkup mid-semester or a pep talk can help. Sometimes, we as students just need someone to vent to. You may not have the answers, but you do have the ability to listen to your child.

7

Remember Your Purpose

Do not expect an easy ride here. Some people are truly gifted in navigating the university system, but they are few and far between. It's going to be hard, especially for a first-generation student since we have many other barriers to face. We have to learn the campus climate from scratch, we can feel like we don't belong at times, we have to search for additional support, we're likely to have financial issues, etc., etc.

But it's okay because our resilience makes us stronger. As long as you refuse to give up and stay focused, you will make it to the end. Remember what you're doing this for and be ready to adapt to any changes that may come in this journey. Life brings its challenges, whether you're in college or not, so you might as well be working for something better in the meantime.

Nothing Good Comes Easy

If this is your freshman year, you may be thinking,

> *"This is all so new and may be hard as hell."*

I'm here to tell you that you are absolutely correct. Unless you are some type of mega-focus, study-king, master sensei, you're going to run into some struggles and complications during your journey. Even if you are a mega-focus, study-king, master sensei, you may still deal with external struggles that many average first-generation students have.

Nothing good comes easy. Easy feats usually don't last forever. Lasting success is built upon a foundation and that takes time to build. But guess what? You have the best tool someone can have—resilience. Let your past troubles turn into positive energy. I personally let my financial and social troubles in my past turn me into an ambitious beast. I felt as if quitting was in no way an option and nothing could stop me, no matter how many times I had to step back a few spaces.

Remember your purpose in life and fight, even when you feel you can fight no more. You have it in you to finish. Trust me. I wanted to quit so many times, but here I am now. It's because I had mentors to keep me going and I let my struggles build my character and heart. Quitting was not an option.

What Are You Doing This For?

Speaking of remembering your purpose, you should ask yourself,

"What am I doing this for?"

Is it money? Are you intending to fix what is broken? Are you working toward a new and better life? There are so many reasons for a first-generation student to take this journey. If you know yours, please remember it. It will be the gas to keep you driving. If you don't exactly know your reason, this is your time to find it. Make it a priority, a mission rather, to find your purpose. Attending college with no purpose can make your college experience a difficult and slippery slope.

I went to college for a better life of course, but I also had a couple of reasons specifically. One reason I chose college as my path was to destroy the vicious financial cycle that plagued my immediate family for too long. I know it seems a bit extreme, and I may be exaggerating a bit, but it is definitely how I felt. Dealing with broken down cars, no electricity, no money for food, no help, and more gave me the motivation I needed to go as far as I possibly could in life.

I remember hearing my mother cry in the other room. I remember working at sixteen years old to keep the electricity on in the apartment unit. I remember only being able to buy bread, eggs, milk, and ramen noodles. I remember rolling up coins in hopes that it would be enough to buy food from the corner store.

I remember thinking I was going through all of this only because my future would be so great. I had a "pay now or pay later" mentality. I had to have hope that I could break that cycle. And although the cycle may not be completely dismantled, I believe going to college and getting a worthy career in education has definitely weakened the cycle. I am now able to take some control back within me, my family, and other loved ones' lives.

Another reason for me going to college was to get out of my environment. I lived in a small, rural town. I saw no hope in staying there. I knew very early that I needed to leave and go to college to have the best chance at a better future. I believed that you had a certain time frame to get out or you would be stuck there, sucked in like a vacuum or black hole. I had to leave the nest. I had to leave my home behind. I've seen people grow old and bitter in my town with not much to show in their lives. Some of them weren't even aware of the opportunities and beauties the rest of the state, or better yet the world, had to offer them. I refused to be that person. I wanted to make the most I could out of life, and staying in my hometown would not get me there.

Although there were so many reasons for me to go to college, one of the last and most important reasons was simply because I wanted to experience life beyond what I already knew. I wanted to see what college was like and maybe get some freedom financially, socially—really in everything. I wanted to start fresh with my life.

These were my biggest reasons to pursue college and were what drove me to not only attend, but finish to get my bachelor's degree. Find what drives you and put the damn key in the ignition.

Plan and Adapt

The absolute best way to remember your purpose and keep your overall goal in mind is by planning ahead and adapting to changes. You may be more skilled in planning ahead, or you may be skilled in adapting on the fly, but both skills can be sharpened and are important in both college and life.

College is not just for taking classes; it is for identifying yourself and picking up useful skills, like communication, networking, time management, critical thinking, and much more. The skills you will develop will assist you in making plans, sticking to your plans, and being competent in adapting to any changes that have to be made. And believe me when I say you will have to learn how to adapt. We can plan all we want, and it is beneficial, but life is not a straight road. You will encounter roadblocks, setbacks, bumps in the road, incorrect signs, ride troubles, and everything else. You must stay resilient, plan to adapt, and overcome.

I experienced many times where I had to adapt or alter plans. I've changed my major twice, was on academic probation, had financial aid and housing issues, and a lot of other stuff that would fill a whole other book if I had time for the petty stuff. But learning to adapt is what helped me push through those roadblocks, which in a way makes adapting more important than planning. You can plan anything you like, but what happens if your plan falls apart? Will you let it crumble and leave or will you figure out a way to build it back up? Never quit. Just adapt.

Don't Give Up

At the end of the day, don't ever give up! Remember your purpose and keep those goals of yours in mind. There will absolutely be times where you are tired, frustrated, doubtful, and maybe even depressed, but do not let temporary feelings stop you from achieving your long-term goals. You must not give in. You must stand tall and take advantage of the resilience you have built in your time. Nothing good comes easy; you must withstand the storms that will cross your path.

So many times I pondered my decision to go to college, wondering if I deserved to be there and wincing at the thought of me not making it all the way. But guess what? I made it. And I don't regret a thing. Stick in there.

Parents

Strive to keep your children motivated. You may be starting to see a small pattern in the role of being college student parents. Your student and future professional will need all the encouragement they can get while they are in school. Check on them every once in a while and try to pick them up when they are down. Show that you care and are willing to do what you can to play a part in your child's success.

Everyone is different, and your child may need different ways of encouragement. I personally needed hard truths and tough love to whip me in shape. My mother gave me grace and hopefulness, which is great, but sometimes I needed a push to get my mind out of the darkness I'd sometimes catch myself in. Your child may not be going through that.

Think about the five love languages: Words of Affirmation, Gifts, Acts of Service, Quality Time, and Physical Touch. These love languages not only apply to romantic relationships, but to any relationship, including that between parents and children. Maybe your child could use an inspiring speech, a gift of something that could help them, or a call out for assistance. Maybe they could use a phone conversation to vent, or an in-person visit if you can. I can't tell you exactly how to support your children, but I can tell you that they need that support.

Help your student stay focused and on the right path. This world is crazy for a young adult going to college, especially for a first-generation student going out to a brand new environment. Assist in making sure they remember their purpose.

8

Take Advantage

There is a plethora of resources on your campus. You don't think so? Look around, go to events, explore and research, and you will find many opportunities to help yourself academically and maybe even financially or personally.

Many organizations, departments, outside sources, and more exist for the benefit of the student. Some may be grant-funded, which means they are supported financially by the government, so they have no reason to trick you out of your wallet. I took advantage of the opportunities I could find to gain academic help, financial aid help, and personal growth. You should definitely avail yourself to the opportunities that are out there for a student. This chapter will discuss some of those resources and what I did to use them.

Talk to Your Professors

One of the most important things to do during your time in college is gain a rapport with your professors. Your professors are humans, not robots. Most of them want that sense of belonging like everyone else. Get in good with your professors for a smoother experience.

This is not a promise that they will raise your grade or let you slack off in class because they like you, but rather a way of networking and relationship building. And who knows, they may actually help you out in the end. It could vary from curving your grade to letters of recommendation for graduate school or even an introduction for a new job or internship. Your professors are a wealth of information, but are often also a wealth of connections. Be sure to not forget that.

I did not recognize or take advantage of this until my very last semester of college. I forgot what class subject it was, maybe a science or history class (I hate them both), but I was struggling heavily. It was around the time of midterms when I started doing the math on my grades (which is a bad idea for your anxiety), and I realized there was barely any hope of passing this class if I continued in this manner. Remind you, this was my last semester, which meant my graduation was on the line. Preparing for graduation and graduate school while also having the overwhelming thought of failure can drive any student crazy.

As I've mentioned before, I was a quiet student. I rarely ever spoke to a professor or made myself known in class. My goal was to be a ghost, learn, and get out. But at this moment, I had no idea of what to do but one thing; I went to speak with the professor.

I remember walking into a faculty building I'd never entered before with a face full of desperation. I didn't know whether to ask for help, admit defeat, or beg for dear mercy when I entered her office. As we spoke, I told her about the situation. She didn't really respond to my anxiety-ridden doom by words, but she did assist me in some of the work and subject matter. I left the office feeling a bit more confident, but still scared as ever. My graduation was at stake.

On the day of the final exam, I took a deep breath as I walked through the door. I had done a math check on my grades again the day before and it was not looking good. Fast forward to when the scores came out. I realized I did not reach the score I needed to pass the class, but it turns out, because I was so close and the professor saw my effort in bringing my grade up, she curved the final grade by just a couple of points so I could graduate.

It was a glorious feeling. I was finally at the finish line, crossing by the hairs of my chinny chin chin. I was able to graduate and continue my life, which would have most likely not been possible if I hadn't swallowed my pride and visited my professor.

Meal Plans

There is a myth that college is an adventure of ramen noodles and Hot Pockets; I wouldn't be lying if I said I would never see them the same because of it. But there is a beautiful campus location that is rarely discussed—the dining hall. Noodles and Hot Pockets are okay, and I grew up on struggle foods, like beanie weenies; beef, rice, and pinto beans; and eggs and rice, etc. But let me tell you, eating at the dining hall on a regular basis introduced me to more varieties of foods than I ever had access to back at home.

I had the pleasure of enjoying both of the University of Houston's two dining halls. One was more basic with the regular American foods and other classic dishes. The other one, the one I visited the most, had a wider selection of foods. They had a stir-fry section, dessert area, fruit section, bakery section, meat station, cereal—everything! There was so much to choose from and many new dishes to try. As someone who did not have access to most of those new foods at home, it helped me open up my taste palette and enhance my cultural competence.

If you can, find a way to get a meal plan. Many universities require you to sign up for a meal plan during your freshman year while in residential housing. This will release your stress levels of finding food and it may open you up to new dishes you've never tried before. You don't have to limit yourself to struggling college student meals. Go to the dining hall at 9 p.m. and enjoy some Froot Loops.

Housing

Yes, housing can be expensive and seemingly unnecessary if you already live in the city where your university is located. It can be a burden when it comes to financing your college education. (I hope you have and are looking for extra grants and scholarships to help with that.) Still, I want to vouch for housing for first-generation college students and tell you why living on campus is worth the possible burden.

First, living on campus makes life so much easier when you are first on your own. Your classes are down the street, impromptu group study sessions are a regular thing, and everything you absolutely need should be no more than a ten-to-fifteen-minute walk on campus. If your university has a bus, you can use it to move around campus; some universities even have bicycle services for easy campus transportation.

Regardless, you move around more freely and efficiently around campus when you are taking advantage of campus housing.

Second, there's a good chance you will gain a greater sense of belonging by staying on campus. According to Maslow's hierarchy of needs, a sense of belonging is the third most important need to us as human beings. Saying that, it can be a challenge for first-generation students to feel as if they belong in a brand new, never before seen climate like a college campus, especially if they are still heavily tied to the environment they grew up in. Staying on campus helps with adapting to the new environment and feeling like you belong there. It may not happen at the first step, but it will grow on you if you intentionally try to experience the campus climate. To support this argument, a research study from Krista Soria & Brayden Roberts shows:

> *The results of the analyses suggest that first-generation students from low-income backgrounds who lived on campus had a significantly higher sense of belonging and higher resilience compared to the matched group of first-generation peers from low-income backgrounds who did not live on campus. Additionally, first-generation students from low-income backgrounds who lived on campus were significantly less likely to report experiencing a hostile or discriminatory campus climate compared to a matched group of first-generation students from low-*

income backgrounds who did not live on campus.[8]

Third, I can't repeat enough how hard it was to deal with the issues at home and still have to deal with issues in school. Housing gave me the ability to escape these issues when I needed to. I could always head to an event, go chill or study somewhere, talk to my mentors at any time, or just simply not be around where the issues prevailed. I've seen associates who have stayed home for college and have had to quit for many life reasons. Staying home was too dangerous for my future. Unless you are going to a community college, which has its own perks, I suggest taking advantage of campus housing.

Counseling Services

Nothing in this book says that college is easy, especially for a first-generation college student. What I am saying is it's possible. One of the things that helped me, and I believe can help you, is professional counseling. Now when I say counseling, I don't mean academic, career, financial, or school counseling. I mean personal, mental health counseling. Just like our bodies need to be taken care of, our minds do too. That's one reason why you're in college, right? It's one thing to learn about your campus, your career, and your major, but it's a whole other thing to learn about yourself.

I highly encourage you to take advantage of counseling services if your campus offers them. The services are often

---

[8] "Living On Campus: Benefits for First-Generation Students from Low-Income Backgrounds" *Living, Learning, & Leading in Residence Life: A Research Study*

tailored for students and paid for under the fees you pay already. You might as well give it a shot.

Let me invite you a bit deeper into my mind state. I personally deal with depression, which was once at a critical state, as well as social anxiety. I found myself suicidal ideation at least twice in my college journey. I had mentors, yes, but it got to the point where they could no longer help me with the skills they had. That's when they recommended I speak to a therapist.

Coming from where I'm from, that was unheard of, something only reserved for crazies. It took me a while to get around to actually accepting the help. I was stuck in my dorm, which unfortunately was more like a mental cell for me. My social anxiety kept me in my room and my depression drove me crazy in there. I went to see a therapist from a counseling department my college provided. I think I paid around $25 and they helped me sort my thoughts and get back on track. Granted, at that time I only went once. I still had my cynicism about therapy. Imagine how much progress would have been made if I kept going. Since then, I continued to take advantage of therapy while in graduate school, and I continue to see a licensed professional therapist in my professional and personal adult journey.

Career Services

If you do not take advantage of the career services department at your college, especially as an upperclassmen (the last two years of college), you are doing yourself a great disservice. Let me remind you that the degree you are seeking is a piece of paper that may get your foot in the door, but it is your responsibility to bust that door open and seek the opportunities ahead of you.

A degree alone does not promise you a job; what you learn and are able to bring to the table after you get your degree is what will get you a job along with that degree.

Career services offers you a plethora of advice, resources, and information to help you thrive beyond your college journey. There's resume building, mock interviews, career counseling, career and job fairs, job databases, and more to keep you updated and looking like someone worth doing business with or hiring.

Let's dive into some of the services I mentioned above. Resume building is simple, but can be tricky based on different situations and job histories. There are career counselors who will help you develop a promising resume. Those career counselors can also talk to you about your options and desires and help you find the best career path. Deciding your future can be highly difficult and you don't want to waste too many credits hopping from major to major repeatedly. Switching majors is common in college, but should be heavily considered!

I switched majors twice during college, once from business to communications and again from communications to psychology. When I graduated high school, I barely had an idea of what I wanted to do. I just knew I had some type of interest in people's behaviors and I knew I had to leave my hometown and pursue something bigger. So, like many confused high school kids, I chose to major in business. Struggling to find a reason for choosing to pursue business, I did research for what type of jobs I could get from a business degree. I found out I could have a job creating surveys and reporting customer trends to companies. Supposedly, it sounds a lot like market research. It only took me about one semester to change my major because I couldn't imagine myself getting suited up every day and playing politics in the business world. Little did I know, politics are everywhere and can't be escaped, but that's a whole other story. Still, I didn't want the life of an average downtown, 34th floor cubicle, businessman, typing my life away. Business is a great and prosperous career, but just not for me.

Then I switched from business to communications because I considered being a radio show host. Today, I don't know why I wanted to do that. I think because I love music so much, but hosting a radio show would probably have made me angry with the way radio and the music business operates. But that wasn't the reason why I changed majors. I found out a popular radio show host in my city had a bachelor's degree in finance. That may not sound terribly unusual, but it blew my naive mind. How did she get a job in the radio industry with a major in finance? While using my resources and research, I deduced that communication majors are much more about networking and playing the field than getting a degree and finding a job. Nonetheless, I chose psychology and stuck with that until graduation. Psychology was the only other major that spoke to me. I remember going through University of Houston's list of majors countless times just to be sure. For me, psychology was the way to go.

I did lose a few credits on the way, but I minimized the damage by talking to my advisor, my career counselor, my mentors, and by doing my own research. Take advantage of your resources before making big decisions.

Mock interviews are fake job interviews that help you get ready for a real experience. You may have done one or two of them in high school. You remember dressing up, preparing to meet with teachers or real bosses, and answering questions in front of them. This is the same thing, but practice makes perfect and a mock interview hosted by career services may be more relatable to a real interview than a high school one. Sidenote, some career services give out information for places to get suit rentals for real interviews if students don't own some themselves.

My social anxiety used to have me terrified of going to job and career fairs, but those events are very helpful. Even if you are not expecting to land a job, these fairs help you significantly with networking and communication skills. Plus, you may learn something new about another career or the career you desire. Make sure you always dress up, come early, smile, and shake hands. And don't be afraid to approach someone. Some companies may actually be looking for a future employee. Know yourself so you can talk about yourself and ask questions. Remember, companies are trying to pay you for your services, so don't be bashful in speaking well about yourself. Just don't seem condescending or conceited.

Tutoring Services

While it is good to work with your classmates, sometimes they can be as confused as you and they aren't enough to lean on for an effective learning experience. Take advantage of the tutoring services on your campus. These tutors can vary from part-time professionals to work-study college students with specific knowledge.

I didn't always go to tutoring; I actually despised it for a while during my under classmen years. I went to a tutoring service once and was turned around for not having enough information to start tutoring. Now I realize I was being ridiculous and asking for too much for them to make something out of nothing, but back then, I thought they did me wrong.

During my freshman year, I had a math class I was completely lost in. I didn't understand a thing! I was way too nervous and socially anxious to ask my professor or a classmate for help. With my back against the wall and my grades in the dirt, I decided to see a tutor. I walked-in with no knowledge of how tutoring worked. In my mind, I didn't expect them to give me the answer, but I honestly did expect some "hand holding." My experience was nothing of the sort. Actually, my experience was nothing.

The tutor asked me what I needed help with and I simply replied,

"Everything."

He started to question me about specific concepts I might have known to get an idea of what to work on. He finally said, and I'm paraphrasing of course,

"I can't help you if you don't even know where to start. Come back when you have specific questions or solutions to work out with me."

I did not go back. I was too embarrassed to. Had I been just kicked out of a tutoring service? I was baffled. Basically, I learned that tutors aren't there to give you the answers, they're there to help in places where you might be slipping. You still have to do the work to understand the subject.

9

Take Advantage Part 2

There's a lot to take advantage of when living on campus and taking college courses. This chapter will continue to point you to opportunities I recommend you look into.

First-Generation Organizations

First-generation student organizations deserve the bulk of credit for my college success. I was in multiple organizations tailored for first-generation students, like the Urban Experience Program and TRIO, which was considered at my college the Challenger Program. As I've said before, this was my home on campus outside of my own dorm. I've learned, laughed, cried, and so much more in these organizations.

First, it's great to have a program that practically does the job for you in finding those who may have similar backgrounds as you. Take advantage of that; make study groups, attend their events, and embrace who you are by becoming a participant with your first-generation peers.

Honestly, I didn't take much advantage of making friends

because of social anxiety, but I did take full advantage of the mentorship. The staff at these organizations welcomed students with open arms and often understood the plight of a first-generation and low-income college student. There were so many times I walked in defeated and then walked out determined. I don't know how I would have made it without their help.

I seriously urge you to search your college for any organizations or programs that cater to first-generation or low-income students. TRIO is nationally known for these reasons and is present at many colleges. These types of organizations come in many shapes and sizes, so be sure to join at least one.

Networking

Networking is essential in the success of your professional career, and college is basically a hotspot for networking. Think about it; you're surrounded by future professionals of all kinds, especially those in your own area of expertise. You never know whom you may benefit from knowing in the future. Even the professors, administrators, and organizational staff are excellent connections to have. The director of the Challenger Program was the person who helped me get my foot in the door for my own profession.

Not only that, but companies and businesses are looking for you. What better place to find you than where you learn? Career fairs, professional seminars, and organizational events can put you in rooms with important people who can assist in your inevitable success. Granted, it's all up to you and no one will determine your path more than you, but ultimately, we cannot tread our journey completely alone and can always use some help. Take advantage of the networking opportunities on your campus. Trust me when I say that they can be the difference between a flop and a flourish.

Recreation Centers

You also have the opportunity to stay active and possibly in shape if your college has recreation centers. The University of Houston recreation center had an indoor and outdoor pool, huge basketball courts, racquetball courts, a climbing wall, and more on the first floor alone. It even had a Smoothie King in it. And the fee for using it was already part of the school's tuition. There was no reason for me to not try it.

My best friend in college at the time, Noel, suggested we workout together at the recreation center. Soon, we had guests and other friends join us. It was easy because the recreation center was usually open late and it was only a couple blocks from our dorms. We came together and pushed ourselves in the name of better health.

College was the first time I tried racquetball, and honestly, smoothies too. I was used to ice pops and cold cups back home, but nothing healthy and refreshing like a cold smoothie after a long work out. But back to racquetball, it was fun and exciting to try a new active activity without having to buy equipment and finding a place to do it. The recreation center would rent out equipment for the students. The climbing wall was a great experience as well. I remember trying it, thinking I was climbing to great heights until I quit. I asked the person managing the wall how far I went, and all he had to do was raise his hand up to show me. Although embarrassing, it was a fun experience.

Overall, I recommend you try out your college's recreation center. It's great for active people and I'm sure people who aren't as active can find something to enjoy there as well. That and we must remember how important physical health is in connection to our mental wellbeing, both intellectually and emotionally. It can help keep the stress down and the energy up for being active in your studies.

Study Abroad

I admit, I do not personally know much about studying abroad because I never participated in one of those programs, but I do wish I had taken advantage of them when I had the chance. Basically, studying abroad is an opportunity to study your courses internationally. Places like Germany, Italy, and England, to name a few, depending on your college's options, are in reach for your academic studies.

Study abroad programs come in many shapes and sizes. Faculty-led programs generally focus on one topic and are structured and controlled by a faculty member at your university. Exchange programs have you enroll directly into a foreign university for you to take classes there for about one year. Focuses in study abroad programs can range from research, language learning, internships, and other basic course subjects.

As a first-generation and low-income college student, I should have taken that opportunity. I may never again have the opportunity to get financial aid to travel to other countries. Granted, there is nothing wrong with not wanting this experience, but if you do wish to travel and learn while doing so, this is an opportunity you can't afford to miss. Check your university for their study abroad options.

Academic Advising

Academic advising is essential to your college success and for graduating on time. Even with mentorship, going to see an academic advisor can be the difference between having everything together and having your college experience slowly fall apart. Let me explain.

Academic advisors are professionals who specialize in their respective academic departments. For example, I was in the psychology program, so I saw an academic advisor from the psychology department. If you want to go into criminal justice, you would see an advisor in the criminal justice department. It's set this way so students have advisors who know all about the programs in their particular department in depth rather than there being general advisors spread thin between all departments. Smaller colleges may not have this privilege, but most universities do.

Because I was on academic probation, I was required to see an academic advisor at some point every semester or I wouldn't be able to register for classes the following semester. I would have gone anyway because the academic advisors helped me keep my course schedule in line and gave me advice on what classes to take next. I learned strategies from my academic advisors regarding course selections and I was able to visually see my path to graduation. This was crucial for me to have a visual representation of my path to help alleviate my fear of the unknown. Even in the times of switching majors, academic advisors played a part in making sure the damage was as minimal as possible in terms of wasting credit hours.

One of the strategies I learned while talking with my academic advisors was to always choose a relatively easy class, a hard class, an elective, and an online class each semester. Of course, this is based on my individual needs, but it does help with a particular issue; it helps you balance your semester. If you have a semester full of classes you consider hard, you can become overworked and stressed easily and risk having a bad semester. If you take all easy classes, your personality and the overall culture of college may leave you too relaxed and you could end up making your classes a lesser priority. Trust me, I've seen it. Also, you'd be leaving all of your harder classes for later. You will hit them at some point and be forced to deal with the issue of having to carry a heavy schedule.

Granted, academic advisors are human too and can possibly mess you up. This is why it's important to stay in control of your schedule and not let the academic advisor do all of the work. They are there to advise, not to baby you.

Professional and Personal Organizations

Last, but definitely not least important, you need to take advantage of the professional and personal organizations at your college. This is a great way to meet people of your kind, network, and gain that sense of belonging you will be searching for when you step into campus culture.

Professional organizations will have you around people who share your career choice and subject interests. These may be people you will run into in your professional life, so it's good to network and make friends with those you feel you can connect and build with. Also, these organizations tend to provide insight and opportunities to jumpstart or advance your career early on. You may be able to get in touch with certain companies and go to certain events that are only available to students in that professional organization.

Parents

Do you and your child a favor and research the college your child is going to. It may be beneficial to search with your child, depending on personal circumstances. You may be surprised at all the opportunities the college has to offer that your child may be ignoring or too nervous to try.

Encourage your children to seek out those opportunities and explore their college for things to learn and grow from. Your child may be too nervous to take that step, so push them to the step, especially in their freshman and sophomore years. Those are often the scariest times as a first-generation college student and also the most important period to get involved. Get them involved!

10

Graduation

You made it! Mostly to the last chapter of the book, but let's go ahead and imagine you walking the stage at graduation. That's the goal, right? The traditional graduation music, the speeches that last too long, the graduation line that mirrors an amusement park. It is a time to cherish as you have truly earned the degree you are about to be handed. Think of all you have accomplished!

Made Yourself Proud

When you walk across that stage, I hope you remember the joys, the struggles, the laughter, and the growth. I hope you re-imagine your new experiences in college in good faith and reminiscence on all the long study times in the library. I hope you do not worry too much about what comes after this milestone and instead bask in the moment as you are about to become alumni of your university. Be proud of your accomplishments. You've come a long way.

Made Your Family Proud

I'm not going to act like I know your family. You may not even be on good terms with your biological family. It happens! But the way I think about it, family is not just biological. Family is whoever you feel is family. And your respected and honorable family members are very proud of you.

Made Yourself a Better You

Throughout your college journey, you will experience changes in your thinking, philosophies, and maybe even religion. You may come out a totally different person. That depends on you. But what I know is you will have made a better version of yourself.

Don't be afraid to learn about yourself. Your self-searching did not end in high school. Honestly, it probably barely started when you graduated high school. Self-actualization will be achieved if you embrace the changes that blossom within you.

Growth is a lifetime of reflection, realization, effort, and change, but the college years are some of the best times to embrace it simply because college life gives you the opportunity to do so. Even if you are working while going to school, maybe dealing with kids, or dealing with general first-generation issues, you are making an effort to change yourself for the better. Appreciation of this is a must once you achieve graduation. You deserve it.

Post-Graduation

So you've thrown your hat, taken your pictures, maybe cried a little, but also graduated college! What's next? Well, you still have work to do. The things I'm about to speak of should have been started around your senior year or your last semester, but I get it, life happens sometimes. Let's go through some of the things to put on your checklist for post-graduation success.

Let me start by telling you now, your college degree does not guarantee you a job. So you ask,

"Then what am I doing this for?!"

Relax, that piece of paper that says "bachelor's" on it will open up more opportunities for you than ever. But here's the catch; unless you strike lucky, those opportunities aren't going to fly into your lap. You have to do what you have to do for professional success.

As I mentioned before, most colleges and universities have career services departments. Talk to the people there and others you trust about your career path plans. Just because you have a bachelor's in one particular subject does not mean you can't curve your path the way you want. For example, I have a bachelor's in psychology, but I used that to focus on a career in education. Some career fields have connections with others if you play your cards right.

Also, make sure to get your resume updated, especially if you have already completed internships or relatable jobs. Do mock interviews to prepare for real interviews. Discuss questions to ask and how to answer specific questions with these interviewers. Learn how and where to apply for jobs, and take advantage of the job fairs your campus may provide for their students and alumni. Look into alumni resources for things like this to stay connected with your university and network.

Don't be afraid to start slow. More than likely, you won't be collecting big checks in your entry-level job. You may even need to take smaller jobs to build experience. After graduating, I took a job advising students which didn't even have a wage or salary. I basically received an allowance. I did that for a year and struggled financially. Luckily, I was accustomed to being broke and could work with it. Some people might think I was settling by taking that job after earning a bachelor's degree. But guess what? That job experience opened more doors and I was able to get into the profession I have now. Getting a job is about networking and getting inside. A lot of the time, once you've successfully infiltrated the world of your profession, you are set.

But maybe you are choosing to elevate your education by going right into a master's program. If so, that's great, but please make sure this is definitely the move you want to make. Graduate school is a big commitment as you may not have the luxuries of free time like during undergraduate school. Also, make sure the path from your bachelor's to master's make sense and you have a plan for what to do with the master's degree.

I made the mistake of rushing into graduate school the very next semester after graduation. I didn't want to waste time, but I played myself because I still didn't truly know what I wanted to do as a long-term career. Six years and three graduate schools later, I'm still working on my master's. I've finally found my way, but I could have saved tons of time and money if I had taken the time to consider my options and made sure the program I went into was right for me.

Lastly, just know you still have a long life ahead of you. You will always have room to learn and grow. Find your role in this world and be the best you can at it. I clearly may not know who you are, but I believe in you. Why? Because as people we are amazing and as first-generation students we are resilient. You will succeed as long as you take advantage of your opportunities, adapt to the challenges at hand, remain faithful in yourself, and stay focused. Let's do it!

About the Author

Terrell Johnican is a poet and author of two poetry chapbooks. He generally writes poetry on life struggles, mental health, and love. He also writes for guidance to the first-generation college student.

Terrell has a B.S. in Psychology with a minor for Media Production and a M.Ed in Higher Education.

He is dedicated to growth and making an impact in lives of the underrepresented people through his career in education, his spoken word, his books, and his business, Highest Caliber Publishing LLC.

You can connect with me on:

- http://hcwriters.com
- https://www.facebook.com/HCWriters

Subscribe to my newsletter:

- https://hcwriters.com/contact-us